The Blind Woman
in the Blue House

Kate Newmann

SUMMER PALACE PRESS

First published in 2001 by

Summer Palace Press
Cladnageeragh, Kilbeg, Kilcar, County Donegal, Ireland

Printed by Nicholson & Bass Ltd.

A catalogue record for this book is available
from the British Library

ISBN 0 9535912 4 7

for
Bridget Anne Ryan

Acknowledgments

Some of the poems in this book have previously appeared in:

Artslink (Belfast 2001); *Cyphers*; *Jobito* (Zacatecas, Mexico 1999); *Papel Poesia* (Zacatecas, Mexico 1999); *Poetry Ireland*; *Quadrant* (Australia); *Roundyhouse* (Swansea 2001); *Seneca Review*; *Sunday Tribune*; *TickleAce* (St. John's, Newfoundland 1999); *Writing Women* (1994); *Word of Mouth* (Belfast 1996).

Some poems have also been broadcast by BBC Radio 2, BBC Radio Ulster and RTE.

'Female Tiger Escapes from Belfast Zoo' was a prize-winner in the PHRAS Poetry Competition, London 1995; 'Let Them Eat Stones' won the Allingham Poetry Prize 1998 and 'At Emily Dickinson's Grave' won the Roundyhouse Poetry Competition, Swansea 2000.

Biographical Note
Kate Newmann was born in County Down in 1965 and educated at Friends' School, Lisburn, County Antrim. Before reading English at King's College, Cambridge, she worked for a year at the Museum of Cretan Ethnology, and learnt Modern Greek. After graduating she taught English as a Foreign Language in Oxford, Cambridge, Rhodes and Belfast. She was a junior fellow at the Institute of Irish Studies, Queen's University, Belfast, where she edited books and compiled *The Dictionary of Ulster Biography* (1993). In 1996 she moved to south-west Donegal. She teaches creative writing, is a freelance editor and a member of the Word of Mouth writing collective.

CONTENTS

At Emily Dickinson's Grave

for Mary Twomey

Already her own chief mourner.

The afternoon dusted with civility,
Sky a slow fermenting sourdough.
I, all skulk and hanker,
Seeking among remorseless skeletons
For her name, at least, in stone.

All that kneading, knocking back.
She'd have known to let it rest
When it found the texture
Of relaxed inner thigh.

What was it I wanted
To know? If there is answer
In the cold hug of perishing earth
After all that yeasty love
Has gone awry?

Her *NO* – I almost heard
That rising wildest word.

Female Tiger Escapes from Belfast Zoo
13th January, 1994

for Ruth Carr

When I need to pray
I look for a miracle
In the water-grey height
Of a heron,
Try not to think of the savage impossibilities
Staring back through bars
At the she-tiger.

Once, with other children
I stood
Repelled by her desperation,
Dulled fur and crazed
Pads indifferent to concrete;
Such a small space that
Every ugly inch was intimate;
Mucous eyes that had met
So many glances
They knew them as a concrete wall.

Only humiliation left,
She hurled herself
From one side
To the other side,
Iron shadows thrown across her back
Like railway sleepers
In sinister animation.

Forwards and backwards,
Careful not to tread a circle,
Defying rhythm and shape,
Jarring and jerking heavy limbs
In case a latent memory
Should betray her into a moment of beauty
Or surrender.

Like a cat ingesting its young
She had absorbed herself
Into this carcass
Which could only keep unstill,
Her own coat caging her.

This morning she is not there.
Men speak of draining the moat
Which stagnated quietly
Around her.

No one says that tigers can swim.

I stifle the growling fear
That she hoped beyond
Her compound for
Another place to be.

I cannot find a prayer for her.
It is winter.
The herons have stayed away.

Reclining Nude
for Sacha

It was a pity, he said, he could not read her poems.
Akhmatova listened as shadows
drummed upon the skin of light
Modigliani stretched across the room
where he choreographed her stillness,
chose precise black
for the curfew of her hair.
Her eyes closed, she saw the squeezed-out paint
harden like a dehydrating slug.
Green, an apple,
halved to reveal an arsenic star,
its own flesh as sky.
Blue was cold-blooded
as the River Neva; a slow vein
of night through the bones
of her city, the touch of its frozen hand.
Modigliani stroked linseed oil
onto her inner thigh,
traced her aureoles like pools
of perfect shade on the pallet
of Parisian noon.
He scanned her line of neck,
drew her nose as careful as a rune,
while, naked, she felt the breath
of her country's dead
escape the pale labyrinth
of the present.

A cat-cry on Montparnasse
reached her as a curlew by the Black Sea.
He had no tone for the loss
that would coffin her eyes
through the swaddling
of long white nights;
no yellow for the few gilt days,
or red for the roses
she hurled in through his upstairs window
    – *They fell so perfectly*   –
leaving their dying colour on his hands.

Let Them Eat Stones

for Michael O'Donnell

they stole our words
we ate seeding nettle
too late on
so it seethed in the gut
it's all in the belly
now we're asked to out-walk winter
the sky breaking down into snow
white as flecks drifting across our nails
white as dull glaze spreading over our delft-blue eyes
white as cow-parsley
a field speckling like this night
yellow-white as white clover
a crop better fed to starving earth
ourselves is all we have to give the grainy clay
white as sheep's wool
we've not woven a long while
white as a rib-cage
like a ravenous jaw
spiking from the hill
like the bones of a boat
wrecked against this cold
white as the white of the egg we remember
its watery knot
all in the belly
white as bleached damask
white as our tongues
white as the raw shapes of air
when it pushes from sore lungs

white as cold skin
white as grey-brown flesh of herring
that's left this shore
vegetable bloody brown of bladderwrack
and carrageen
we've tried to eat it all
haunted white of an empty net
white as bog-cotton
cuckoo-spittle at the corner of a human mouth
white as the scraped stomach of an animal
white as inner shell of periwinkle
when you've picked the small meat
white as poor flour
white as hawthorn
white as bird skull
chalked of its rotten body
by sharp water
singing a dead wind
white as tooth
white as gum
white as knuckle-bone
white as gristle
white as cabbage-moth
white as snow-berry
white as our stare
white as the stones which hold sickness
white as dandelion clock done telling
white as the milky circle of its broken stem

white as the flat wet eye
of a halved potato
before it took the blight
white as down
white as the lough
is black
its quiet sediment
all in the belly

Rachel's Lament

for Kerry Hardie

And Laban said,
It must not be so done in our country,
to give the younger before the firstborn.

Not that I am wishful
For locusts in Jacob's heart
Or drought in Leah's cool sister eyes,
But what have I?

What have I but promise,
As he wears his marriage
Like shoes which grow
To fit his feet?

He and she are trained vines
Lacing the scuffed earth
With mutual shadows

And I, in my grove of grief,
Forever losing ground.

My breath onion-heavy with questions
Whose answers reek,
Thistledown in my throat,
Brain an angry artichoke.

Just as he whittles
Almond, medlar,
Carob branches – his beautiful
Supple hands – he is paring away
His need of me.

Mouth full of must,
I pillow my head
On ashen stones, lichen-grisled,
Bleached of forgiveness

And chafe against
Rough-woven night;
Convolvulus and nettle,
Asphodel and silence seeding.

By day my misery
Settles in sunlight;
Rancid vinegar mottling good oil.
In the dark reach of his eyes,
Wild anemone, cyclamen, oleander:
In mine, a harvest of tares.

Theirs are the seasons.
Ells of thunder folding over us,
Torrential guttering rain,
Smoulder of olive-stone fuel,
Crushed kernels glowing ochre,
The muted moon tapering its light.
She ages him.

I watch him at his husbandry
– sheep ringstraked as our love –
And I spit out the unleavened days,
The husk of his want.

Sifting thirty types of tears in my sleep
I dream a kestrel as a speckled angel,
Slaking the air,
Shaking the light off her wings;

I dream the last rung of a ladder,
Truth ending there.
I gather firelight in a colander:
Lust another seven years.

Endless Chrysanthemums

for Feargus McGarvey

Your script half way to picturing, one line became
A bank of honesty leaning into mist.
I miss days when you would send
Knapweed, ragwort, yarrow,
A scribble, a sketch,
Definitive grasses, defiant delphiniums,
Startled sunflowers,
The frailty of a tulip petal
Leeched by rain.

Eclipse

for Walt Kilroy

It is a dull coin
On the burning tongue of sun,
Ferrying us into what we already knew:
The dark remembered failure
Of our loves; the acrid
Aftermath of when and why:
A black wart blotching a healthy leaf;
A tumour like an ink blot
On the brain's x-ray, tangling
All the threads of light;
Trepanation of the universal skull;
A stopper in the bottle-neck of time;
The ultimate eye, shutting itself
Against pity.

Etowah Indian Mound

for Marilynn Richtarik

Etowah takes the sun into sleep.
Its smoky light is all a signal.
Its rivers have sunk back.
It is a land-bound island
Beached in fertile silt.
Etowah has let the meanness drain away;
Is serene as the half-moon on a child's fingernail.

We, like gar or catfish,
Have narrowed in our living,
Trapped in a weave of trivia.

Etowah teaches
You cannot swallow
A skyful of clouds
For a mouthful of spit.
You can't take fire
And give back air.
You can't cage the wind
With wires.
You must allow the river
To be fragile as a human spine.

Etowah is part of us
We let go before we could
Give it a name.

Its own name, E T O W A H,
America has forgotten what it means,
Or never cared to know.
e t o w a h
Is like whispered breathing,
Or the sea told inland through a shell.

Etowah is the god
We place out of reach.
Etowah is the lull we long for
In rain we danced for:
The answer we drown out
In chanting the question.

A fence holds our latticed stare,
Our pale hair, dry-leaning grass,
Unmoving shadows of sweetgum,
Sourwood, hackberry.
The mesh is a dream-catcher
For Etowah,
Keeping out the nightmare of us,
Our want.

Reclamation

I was thinking of the Zuider Zee

        When your sister told me

Its salt-tamed, cold-bordered blue

        That you had gone to Holland

Of Elvira on a bus from Lelystad hospital

        You were living with a woman

Her husband was ill

        You had told your wife and son

She was having to sell her precious stone collection

        You had never felt so free

She had told her husband

        Free from past and future

She hated the polders

        And you had left for Holland

It was unnatural

        To live with a young woman

Sooner or later the land would sink back

        For good.

Pasiphae Sat, Old and in Black

for Athena Skordalakes

I was young
and very beautiful.
If you had seen –
breasts like lemons,
Minos used to say.
Very beautiful.

But…thus it ends.
I saw the bull
and I loved that moment.
I loved him, the way he was.
I understood Europa well then.
Beautiful, white
with long eyelashes above
his big eyes,
and soft skin
on his chest, between his legs.
If you had touched.

Well, I said to him,
I love you, but he didn't understand.
He didn't understand
because a bull he was.
Thus, to have him
I had to become a cow.
Eh…

They made me a cow

with wood and I got inside
but I didn't like it.
Very hard. My knee
hurt the way I was.
And it smelt of resin.
My smell couldn't be smelt
and I couldn't be seen.
But I waited, I waited.
I couldn't
go to him. I couldn't.
I could only stand like that –
wood.

And he came, and he got on top of me
but I didn't feel anything.
Only his thing.

I couldn't touch the fur
on his chest or stroke
his eyelashes
or hold onto his horns
which I had thought would be good.
And quickly it ended.

Nor the white could I see
and I only faintly heard
hot breath from his soft nostrils,
like silk.

And I was beautiful, but
a bull he was and he didn't understand.
Wood I had to become in order to have him.
He only loved the wooden cow.
But if I hadn't got in
he would have crushed me likely.

Eh…thus it is.
And I had the child, bad fate,
and it was not well.
Μα…αν θελουν οι θεοι…
Τι να κανουμε;
But…if the gods want…
What can we do?

Giorria

I would talk to you
outside the heaviness of hearing.

I would make with you
sign language for turtle,
belly a carapace along your back,
safe everywhere swimming.

Like sanguine hawthorn
I'd have you knowing
before the weather broke.

I'd wish for us wisdom
of the one who takes no name,
thundering into another language
out of our sight.

I'd give you my birthmarks
to savour like grounds of fine roast coffee,
read like tea-leaves,
Ursa major, Ursa minor,
musical braille,
nerves for quavers and rests;
your limbs and mine
treble and bass clefs.

I'd write it as a black snake in Sicily
signing with its inky self
off the page,

its own lettering all
it wants to say on earth.

I'd have us learn how
a gentle touch on a larynx
can tell the word from its fibre
and its stalk.

I'd say it was wild:
storm carding a clump of sheep's wool
on bramble;
noiseless as tree frogs
brought from nowhere
by hot pockets of huge rain.

Out-running Haley's comet
I'd hurtle into Orion's open arms,
unlistening to shouts of dead light.

At the Agora
for Margaret O'Beirne

Margaret said she wouldn't go there alone.
We acted our age,
doubting each other's sense of direction
and our own.
I clutched her bag
while she shouted shoe-size
across market-reaching arms.

I bought dried garlic
and bunched basil with roots,
soil wrapped in paper
sogging through words, through garlic husks,
putting back the living wet.

We stopped at a fish stall,
paid obeisance, gawping at
heftiness of eels
spelling Sargasso in spilt mercury:
all the disappointed distances,
a chill silver meal.

We stood our ground
eyeing the hacked torso
of a landed tuna,
a cross-section of slung flesh, round
bone, a single glaring eye.

Glimpsed through shoals of people,
their mammal movements,
a dish of quiet shifting clams
kissing bubbles, shocking as labia.

We fled this trinity of animal, mineral, vegetable,
to wrap our eyes in cotton remnants,
sunflower abstracts and yellow child-drawn fish.
As Margaret bought two for table-cloths
because of their brightness, the bells
of a nearby church – St. Agatha's –
rang and Margaret said
she wanted to go to Mass.

Afterwards she mentioned
the smell of my garlic
had put her off her prayers.

Wisteria Day

for Nunzio and Carmen

A morning on Via Regina Margarita
Makes you think of other streets
Which aren't as broad as daylight;
Where bookstalls don't scatter James Joyce's *Dead*
Among Sicilian recipes for ptarmigan soup,
Baked Sicilian quail, the Sicilian quail almost extinct;
Where a row of windows, like a strip of negatives
Doesn't frame mannequin torsos
In wedding dresses, shroudal off-white;
Where fallen bougainvillaea
Doesn't bank like dying confetti,
Or the Indian fig protrude
Its prickly pears like private anatomy;
Where wisteria, grown lugubrious,
Isn't trained across the yard like a huge weary elbow
Supported, unwieldy on a stool,
Tired of propping grandeur through hot Sicilian afternoons;
Where no foreign soldier smiles gratitude
For the offering in a currency still meaningless to me:
For him, measured against the weight of space
Where his left leg should be, its ache perpetual.

Coming to on Mount Etna

for Carmelo Zaffora

This place is forgetting us as we breathe.
It mystifies us, respecters of its madness,
in a cold vapourish sulphuric blur.
Glad to tread on the reptile rocky skin
of its unpredictable, ungrateful
wilderness, uncaring of how loss
shrinks the shape of air in the slow cooling.
There is snow where we looked for molten welter,
peering sky-ward for singed cloud,
some telling whorl of smoke, a geological finger-print, a broil.
Only a cold steaming and chamomile smelling rank, unlike itself
and the lichen and the broom decomposing
into broken soil, noiseless, and no birds.
And we, not right knowing ourselves
step awkwardly, as on clinkers,
black lava like carbonised sugar.
We gather chunks, first-footers into a new
confusion of temperature and time,
guileless as people who have purchased the moon
and hold meteorites to prove it.

Espresso

for the woman in Gangi who wouldn't serve me
coffee because the boss was away getting change

She stood firm
behind her black apron
behind the cappuccino machine
behind the high counter
like a nurse in a morgue
adept with innards
but forbidden from incising
without supervision.

She shook her head,
eyes magnified –
misshapen through lenses
thick as the bottom of a wine bottle –
looking into mine
as though she could teach me a thing or two.

Fairgreen

in memory of Adrian Lamph

No words passed between us.
He worked at the Fairgreen,
A bleak, grey, tarmacked place
Where skips of record-players,
Bed-heads, fine unhinged wooden doors
Made a litany of waste,
A lie of need.
From a distance
We saw him salvage a white cot.
And just to know
His long, shining pony-tail,
His cheek-bones in the light,
To learn
Post-peace
That he was knee-deep
Among cut grass
When an unnamed man
On a bicycle
Ended him
With no words passing between them.

Rime

Maybe it was my ghost
Startled from the hedgerow
Along the road to Carrickmacross
Where a single blackthorn
Halted my gory separation
From her, four years before,
And just the same, the
Worst time of the year.

Coming to in the hostile
Beauty of your dark eyes
Which cannot hide,
She didn't say
What she'd intended;
To remind us of a day
When you might not have been there
And I might not have been there.

Was it my ghost,
Wondering why we punish
Our bodies so with sorrow,
When even the hawthorn
Foretells the bitterest cold?
It goes ahead and risks its sanguine berries
Along the deepest ditch.

The Blind Woman in the Blue House
for Ann McKay

Between open-eyed lilies,
azucenas, white,
a blind woman combs the blue house:
sandstone nalgas, snake wood on the hearth,
parched ceramic frogs dying for lack of atl.

Could she hear the hot-night blues, the cicada ochres,
the whites of eyes, the greens of unripe figs?
Could she know the long-dead space
weighed down with old turtle,
its canvas skin, its smooth dead shell
an artefact, without the painted pain
of Frida's plaster corset?

Could she guess the genius;
lip-read the place
from the Toltec slant of stone mouths,
hard as mixing the colours of blood and sun,
or smell promiscuous the conchs
embedded in the wall?

Did she sense, upstairs,
Frida's empty wheelchair,
the unfinished painting of Stalin,
as though, on his collapse,
Frida alone had dared,
risen to her feet
and rushed to Stalin's side?

Oh, the blind woman in the blue house,
through the parrot-shrieked colours
she could taste the sorrow
of all that could not be touched.

Debit and Credit
for Uriel Martinez

In the Museo Diego Rivera
I had a vision of Guadalupe:
Guadalupe Marin, divinely dark;
her daughter, Guadalupe Diego Marin
clasped in holy robes on her mother's knee.
In the picture also, Diego;
their embossed wallpaper.

Frida Kahlo's icon of Guadalupe Marin: the thickness we become.
Lupe revealed to her, the second wife, recipes
for Diego's favourite dishes;
just how he liked them.

In Frida's house, the account book lists
Income: Diego's total; Frida's;
Expenditure: staples, tips, electrical goods
and
Extras Diego:

To Lupe Marin	March	200 pesos
	April	300 pesos
	Loan	100 pesos
	TOTAL	600 pesos

Los Toros
for Cary Monreal

I am told
the worst thing in the wild
is to find yourself with a lonely bull.

I have seen a dead bull
lying by the road-side,
its shoulder blades
like someone in a trusting sleep.

Just as stone memorises warmth,
gentle brick arches
of a disused bull-ring
echo hooves, echo hooves.
Red geraniums in tiers
where generations sat.

I am told how bullfighters
help at the birth of calves,
their only chance to know
what they must love at one remove
until they come to harm.

I am told how
the intact places of the earth
are kept for rearing fighting bulls;

saved from cropping the harrowing heat;
spared indignities of crude-cut horns
healing over, pappy like broken cactus.

I am handed back the guilt,
reminded of the ugly state I live in,
its complex violence, its hideous sacrificial simplicity;

till all the words
are screaming from the sun
and from the shade.
I am encircled, betrayed
by the unfamiliar,
bound to honour
iconographies of blood.

And I am crying imperceptibly
as I am told bulls do;
dust in my nostrils,
the constellation Taurus like textured wax
drowning in a wash of night,
the horned moon gone
but turning somewhere, lurking
to fell me with the whole body
of black sky.

Unfinished Woman

for Alfonso Lopez Monreal

Paint me very pregnant;
a dark sun, brilliant
with knowing I carry Santo Nino,
will keep him unscathed by my discovery
of *In the beginning was the Word.*
Make me all chiaroscuro
and guarded against language.

Or Montezuma's daughter.
Colour me cold on the Sierra.
Water down my breath to thin silver.
Show my Spaniard holding out to me
as gift, what was already mine.

Maybe Sor Juana Inez de la Cruz,
but clothe me back in my real name:
Juana Inez de Asbajey Ramirez de Santillana. Red.
No cool churchy colours,
no celibate greys.
Have me naked in the garden,
rewriting all the books of Mexico
on adobe walls
and paint God with me
as a splitting fig, or as a pinking tunas.
Don't show me dying alone of fever,
denied by those who most feared love.

Or Juana Gallo, drunk on the Cathedral steps,
Zacatecas falling away from me
in pinks and churrigueresques.
I'll be no old baroque.
Show my dogs attentive,
of all the eyes around, theirs the most intelligent.
Paint me with my basket,
Pancho Villa cradled inside.
Show the seduction of real anger.

Or la mujer del huevo, the egg woman.
Lying back inside the outline of my shell,
an albumen moon which has swallowed the sun,
the substance of my own tempera.
Mix me the colour of papaya flesh.

I am a visitation. I am the Virgin of Guadalupe.
My hair is night, draped in deep-water dusks, burning blues.
My eyes are wide skies.
My skin is your skin.
My hands in prayer have held us all.

Dream of a Portrait Painter on a Sunday Afternoon in the Alameda

for Ben and Anna

I am failing him, I know
From the people who stop to stare.
He makes me look straight at him.
We are an arm's length apart
In his booth.
His face creases to an intricate grid
Moving to map my features.
I can see backwards
Through his plain glass glasses,
Thick black frames
Worn, like Martin Luther King's,
From need to give his vision weight
In the eyes of the world.
I sense sadness settle on my face.
He grapples in his pocket,
Rubs out the last line.
All his money is in his sock.
He gives me my change,
Says I am like a saint,
Crossing himself, signs his name, Flores,
And hands me my portrait
Of someone else.

Last Will
for Cathal Ó Searcaigh

For the journey to Lopez Velarde,
drive to Jerez
across the dry river,
its algaed, lichened bed
a green watermark
on the papery desert.
The town makes no concessions.
Doctor, dentist, three opticians,
library, school, two obstetricians,
Frenos and Clutch,
two halves of raw cow
hung unflinching,
a pail of animal guts, heavy
and Ramon Lopez Velarde's house
holding a pose,
pink distemper peeling
like cheap rouge.
Inside, the walls
barely hide their black and white,
their sepia aspirations.
Enter the rooms – cool spaces
sculpted by the scent
of warm orange-blossom
filtering from an inner yard.
Stop at Lopez Velarde's Oliver type-writer
Latina Number 13, unmoved.
He took E,I,S,T,O with him,
the keys worn to anonymity,

left speechless.
Let the day stretch you
into sound, wind words
into heat.
Look down Lopez Velarde's well,
see your own fatigue reflected
in the scummy disc of standing water.
Tread softly into the private places,
the intimacy of his kitchen,
cooking pots upturned like hats,
the termite-laden shelf
the only meal there's been
for years. Don't startle the pigeons
who'll come like symbols
or like spirits to scrutinise.
They've left the bathroom
full of bird-shit
but you can still
watch your whole height
inside the gilt margins
of the parched mirror.
There are pots of arum lilies
open wide as though declaiming poems,
megaphones you cannot hear.
Nothing breaks the silence
of the bedroom – don't stay there
too long.
But pass into the good room,

his parents' photograph
and three Virgins of Guadalupe,
a quiet gramophone, some crochet,
a quieter piano lacquered black.
Return to the inner yard,
the orange tree a canopy of musk,
a vanilla almond sky,
a limbo of sensibility.
Walk around it slow, the orange
will be there for you,
a bright cobble that has worked itself free,
its fullness and its breathing skin,
holding a distillation of the river
which like Lopez Velarde
will never see the sea.
He died when he was thirty-three
of bronchial pneumonia.
He leaves you this.

From La Quemadera to La Quemada
for Daniel Dultzin

Pale in the Quemadera,
The place of Inquisition,
San Diego's flame-dark domes
Sprouting crosses like vines
Fed by the urine and the blood.
Fire fades to an anaemic retablo
There in the Alameda;
Jacarandas snowing mauve.

In ancient La Quemada, Xochimilco,
Among the cacti
Charred by unexpected snow,
Cacti crying huge vegetable tears
For the spiders, cicadas, the birds
Consumed by cold
And the cacti themselves
Slumped on fences like war-dead
Or blackened free
Against the heretical sky
As though the burnt
Of the Inquisition
Pushed up from ash and dust
To stand accusing,
Waving in their phantom limbs
The scorched and sooted books of Indian lives.

At the museum
The long dead have become
Their own temple of skulls,
Dangling their crania,
Their long-bones, like puppets
Learning to dance 'Los Santiagos',
Jangling on the wind.

On La Quemada, the wind
Telling
And telling you
Against your skin.

Hannah
for Gordon and Elma

My life was one unclean issue.
I drank so much
red wine for the consummate
fire it allowed in the bones
and the dulling of those
worst truths, till I was
estranged from my own hair.
Even the fruits
frightened me, ripening each other
off the tree.
But roots and vegetables would not soften
their woody core
for all the heat and waiting
I could give.
The days spilled into what I ate.

Until the Lord brought Fire.
Unlike the theft of ember
from one side of log to another,
all my skin
was alive with hunger;
the body a bark
discovering its shore-line,
all hankering subdued
to a soft warm ash.

Oh Samuel, Samuel,
can the Lord be just fire:
cleaner than flesh;
void without its destruction;
all its smell, its sound,
borrowed from what it burns?
There was nothing I could tell you
of why I had to leave you.
And now I offer up to you
a coat a year to gird you
and pray to barren earth
that I suckled you enough,
– a taper dipped and dipped in my tallow –
to recognise God in your own voice.

And I cannot forgive fire:
the bursting juices of the brain
boiling till skull is trap;
the copper flame licking at the wounds,
a lie in its leap of blue;
the idols it sculpts too quick,
too hot to hold in memory.
Even the charring wood knotted with sad eyes
peering from the grain,
wrapped in flame's lascivious sinews,
hissing as it finds song in burning,
'til smoke becomes the smother
we watch each other through.

The Tony Tanner Memorial Lecture
for Stephen Coles

This morning
King's College Cambridge
are auctioning the books
of Tony Tanner
long-time Fellow
his first editions
copies signed
with love.

What happened
to his humidifier
his healthy indoor plants
his Persian rugs
his antimacassar
his bronze nude
his cat?

Moonambel

for Eileen Graham

Dear Aunt, wrote Dorothy
to her aunt who had reacted so,
riled against her lonely wanderings.
There were limits.
She bundled the letter into her bag –
blue and red embroidered, little Christmas trees,
or aimless arrows in interlock,
like she and Willy –
the post-bag which wandered with her
into Ambleside with Willy's poems
for the world.

His tall-brimmed straw hat
pristinely set off his gentle head.
Willy thought the red and cream silk
fetching when she lovingly looped it
round his brim.
How would anyone understand?

The day he left her she lay
in vacant or in pensive – no, passive – mood,
her senses held at bay,
stifling the images she had borne for him;
lay on her back breathing only the thought
of his voice in Germany pouring the lines
out into Alpine air
for both of them; a distillation of the lakes.

She would fill her letters with account of him,
his stanzas spilling off her parchment.
Willy could reason against monarchy,
chasten himself with a gentle
*But let us speak no more of * * *.*
For her the words rolled on
gathering momentum until she reined in,
and went sensibly back to bury them
with broad strokes of her iron-base ink.

She had worn his ring until today,
when he came to her room and slid it from her finger,
the light quartered through cottage glass.
For a moment, he found her hand and slipped it back,
but now, it was binding him to a woman from Penrith
and she was lying stiff on the bed spread

where she had thrown herself, hardly knowing her own place.
Her face assumed the smooth-cheek contour of a death mask
till warning came that the bridal party from the church
approached, and she raised up like Lazarus.

Gazing from the window,
she sickened at the shrinking shadows,
the black ebbing out of the lake:
its anger she had learned to respect,
but now the sun had coaxed and cajoled,
dark honesty had given way to a dubious glow.

Stricken

Is it like
the wild sea-heave
landing needlessly
a mass of fish
on Muckross hill,
their dead weight cleaving
to the earth and to their feather bones?

The only words I have
trickle like accidental rain
into my mouth.

You, journeying in Majorca
where George Sand and Chopin
took shelter in a rented house.
Lime walls became a damp lung
but Chopin wrote of
palms and cedars, cactuses, olives,
lemons, aloes, figs and pomegranates
and you took cuttings
from their garden,
slipped Majorca back to Ireland,
dug in the heels
where they might grow their song
through layers of unaccompanied light,
because you have the language
and know about geraniums
and wintering.

Sea-Change

for Mary Sexton

If I must say something now,
Though it matters less,
Let it be to thank you
This frost-defined day,
Colder than Moscow,
For restoring my rapport
With the surfaces of winter.

I can stop now
Straining to hear through turf ash
What is being sung
By burning log, bark and moss;
Stop finding seal-song
In the emulating crawk
Of sea-abiding rooks
Long after the seals have left.

Bathsheba

for Eilish Martin

I, in the eye of the beholder,
drawn to David by desire.
Sometimes we cannot tell
its pull from the call
of Jehovah.
He drew me out of many waters.

Clutched in the shadow arm of time,
his belly to mine,
the heat of touch
in waves against
the gently shelving truth.
All night made we his bed to swim.

I knew our child at once,
burning wild cherry red:
an angel told me.
How David must have known
before our breath was rent apart
like red sea.

Then, falling in my eyes,
he made himself kin
to a new kind of anger,
white and cold as angel wing.

I charted myself in his disregard,
a waxing moon
pushed back from night

to the glare of an indifferent sun.

He'd have coupled Uriah to me,
trundling, yoked, into oblivion.
And I'd not have prayed for Jehovah's help
if I had thought
his hot displeasure could forge such an end.

Golden calves run amok
and Uriah, hoof-marked,
comes to me in dream,
his throat an open sepulchre.
My sorrow is continually before me.

I, a valley of death,
warding off still waters
till the child was born;
swaddled for the tomb;
his days just a handbreath.

Now David walks in his integrity
and has his Lord as his Rock.
I mend myself for Solomon
Jedidiah, my second son,
and do not say,
when David offers up
The wicked are estranged in the womb
why, in the mouths of babes and sucklings,
I hear YAHWEH as a hollow cry.

Lobsters Die at 44°C

for Ciarán McBrearty

Their antennae
bent and broken,
their wild eyes as we plunge them
into tepid salt water
to lure them from themselves.
The lobsters' gleam, their blue-black
and struggle, the degrading clamour
against the pan, and once
they seemed to turn on each other;
we don't know
if it was territorial
or fierce response to pain.
After stillness settles
their dying water
holds the stench of drowning,
poured away
before we add the Santorini wine,
its bouquet of black soil
white rock with vines rooted in dust
a white distance from the sea
and the dry suck of sunlight.
The final steaming – onion, carrot, thyme,
juniper berry – leaves their perfect shells
naked as molten magma,
marbled as cold-chafed hands,
measled as skin by an open fire.
Claws held out, a gesture of defeat.
Flesh like moonlight,
an ebb on the tongue.

Van Gogh's Brother, Vincent
for Sally Wheeler

The weaver in the turfy dusk
Bowing his labouring back
To lean into his wooden loom
As though it were an upright piano
Lacquered by the window's melancholy beam;
The worn shuttle a strong heart beat
Through the cool warp of camphored silence:
The artist's hungry pulse no match
For its unfaltering staccato song.

To have a brother die before you
With your name must be like
Sitting at that loom in the mean light
Of your own disregarded picture
As your fingers feel the pattern
Forever pushing through from the other side.

Retablo

for Alaska Adriana Veldt

Graphite on pages torn from last year's books.
Class after class on the floor of the library.
'If you can't write, draw,' their teacher shouts.
I am the day my daddy was killed.
I am the day my brother shot two rabbits
with one bullet.
I saw a car burnt out.
The boy beside me, intent,
sketches a big rectangle;
on it a large round body,
spidery stick figures standing by,
and tells me his grandfather in hospital
just before he died.

I am taken back to Plateros, Mexico,
cloisters hung with need
and gratitude, painted on wood, on card, on paper,
that cusp of desperation
caught in colour: a kneeling pilgrim,
a hank of hair,
a child's plaster-cast and shoe,
the clearest edges to our human outlines.

Another child can only whisper
when I kneel beside him.
His picture of a dog solid grey,
as hard as the pencil could lean,
I remember when my dog died
with a puppy inside her.

Oh Santo Nino, what can I draw
to give them the miracle of themselves:
the children of Barrack Street Primary –
stick figures with pencils
on a library floor?